BIKING

Written By:
Herbert I. Kavet

Illustrated By:
Martin Riskin

© 1992
by **Ivory Tower Publishing Company, Inc.**

Manufactured in the United States of America

---

30 29 28 27 26 25 24 23 22 21 20 19 18 17 16 15 14 13 12 11 10 9 8 7 6 5 4 3 2 1

Ivory Tower Publishing Co., Inc.
125 Walnut Street
P.O. Box 9132
Watertown, MA 02272-9132
Telephone #: (617) 923-1111   Fax #: (617) 923-8839

"It's nice being in a place where you don't have to lock up your bike."

"Those titanium bikes really are light."

Mail Order Catalogs

The minute you show any interest in biking, a secret society sends your name to Performance or Bike Nashbar and they start sending you bike catalogs about every 3 hours. The prices are really great in these catalogs but there is this ethical dilemma about buying from them or supporting your local bike shop. Do not worry about this. Everyone buys from these catalogs but when the various parts arrive, 90% of the cyclists can't put them on their bikes. Bike shops make a fortune assembling things embarrassed people bought in catalogs.

"Well, I think it would be cheaper if you bought
a stationary bike like other people."

"Cynthia has been searching all her life for
a downhill century."

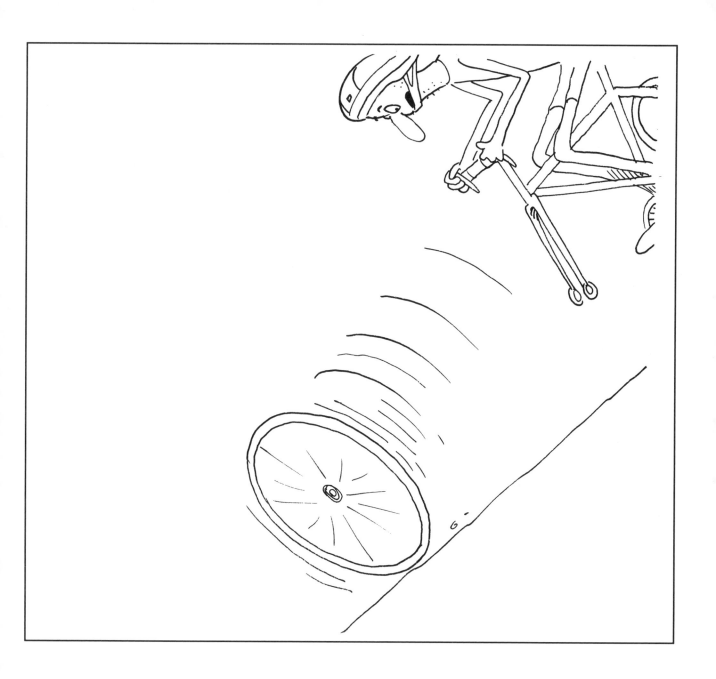

"Now, did I tighten those quick releases?"

Handling Dogs

The perfectly lovable doggy that licks your face when you're off your bike, turns into a growling bloodthirsty monster when you pedal by. No one knows the reason for this. If you're going to cycle, you're going to be attacked by dogs and you'd better memorize these 4 methods of handling dogs or you're going to go to work Monday morning with a whole lot of teeth marks on your body.

Handling Dogs

1. You can out run them, which is much easier if you're riding downhill.

2. You can bring your own dog along and hope they will be so busy sniffing each other that they'll leave you alone.

3. You can stop and get off your bike, at which point the very confused animal will turn back into a lovable doggy, but then, of course, you'll never get anyplace.

4. You can carry some sort of spray deterrent but by the time you get it out, most dogs will already have eaten you.

"Gene's bike was only 19 lbs. when he started."

"Sam is so conscientious about his hydration."

Why The Wind Is Always Against You

Every biker quickly notices that the wind is not your friend. It is always pushing against you. Common sense would seem to indicate that at least half the time the wind would help you, but this is not so. The reason is VECTORS. When the wind is directly against you, the vectors push against you and slow you down. When the wind is from the side the vectors interact with your apparent speed and also slow you down. It's a common fact that the wind is never at your back and this probably has something to do with vectors also. I don't understand this either.

Bikes and Cars

Although, in the interest of fuel economy, cars are getting smaller and smaller, most are still bigger than a bike and the source of most cyclists' anxiety. I mean look how the meekest accountant turns into a homicidal maniac behind the wheel of an X-3000 something. Think of the potential for a pickup driving redneck whose girlfriend has hidden his beer. I mean I have horror stories of truck–bike encounters that if printed here would absolutely kill all sales of this book.

Bikes and Cars

There are three basic methods to avoid being run over by cars.

1. Ride only on bike paths where <u>you'll</u> run over the Roller Bladers.

2. Wear bright colors so the police and ambulance can find you in the drainage ditch.

3. Stay way to the side of the road to improve the chance of a glancing blow rather than a bone crushing one.

"Oh no, <u>we</u> can't ski like everyone else."

"Honey, have you seen my biking gloves?"

Traveling With A Bike

A whole industry has grown up providing racks to attach your bike to your car. This enables you to project a healthy outdoorsy image while not really having to pedal too far. Some people just buy the racks and skip the bike part entirely. They get to their destination even faster. Traveling by plane with a bike is an experience you don't want to know about.

Traveling With A Bike

If you have a newish car you're going to want to give a lot of thought to the bike rack 'cause bikes have lots of sharp pointy edges which destroy your car faster than salted roads in New England. Roof racks avoid most of this problem but, of course, you need a hydraulic lifting device to get the bike on or off.

"I can't stand women who show off."

"Me? I'm in life insurance."

Racer's Nightmare

Every racer and, to a lesser extent, every cyclist that rides a swift looking road bike, has a reccurring nightmare. It involves being overtaken and passed by a mountain biker peddling in sneakers and jeans, without an aero helmet and smoking a cigarette.

If you're a guy, hopefully you'll wake up before the part where you realize that this Mountain Biker is a girl.

"Don't be ridiculous. There are no PIRANHA in this part of the country."

"It's one of the most comfortable bikes I've seen."

Hills & Stop Signs

Why is there a stop sign at the bottom of every good hill? I don't know about your neighborhood, but anytime I hit 35 MPH I also get ready to hit the brakes. It would seem much more sensible to have the stop signs at the top of hills.

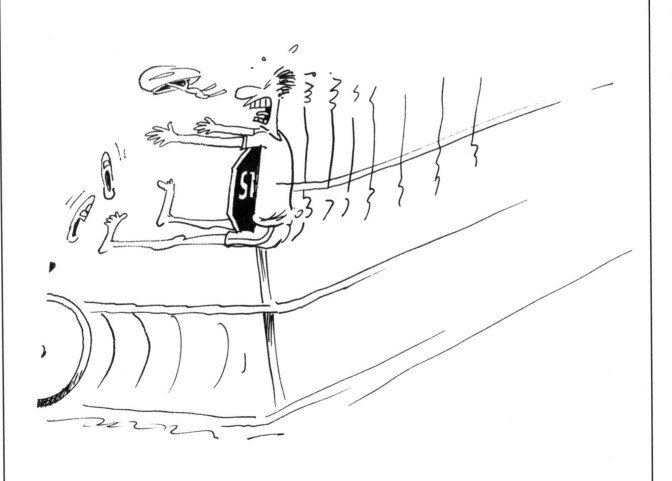

"Well if beer does that to your digestive system, <u>you</u> should ride in back."

If dogs could really catch bicycles.

"I see you got new clipless pedals."

Why All Bikes Weigh The Same

You buy this 18 lb. carbon fiber–titanium studded beauty for about the price of a small Japanese car. Surely you can't park this treasure by a tree and just leave a "Do Not Touch" note on it. Oh no, you need a Super Kryptonite guaranteed lock that weighs about 8 lbs. plus the bracket to haul it around.
Total weight 27 lbs.

Your average "Made in Taiwan" steel welded bike may tip the scales at 26 lbs., but no one is going to steal it so you can secure it to the lamp post with a twisted piece of wire.
Total weight 27 lbs.

N.Y. CITY BIKE SAFE DEPOSIT PARKING

When bees fly into helmet vent holes.

"These tandems certainly pick up speed
going down hill."

"The pink meat was delicious, but I can't get any marrow out of these bones."

Bike Shoes & Cleats

The idea of bike shoes and cleats is to improve your biking efficiency by fixing your feet to the pedals so you can pull up as well as push down. This gets a whole new set of muscles sore. You can also get home much faster which enables you to plop down sooner in front of the TV with a beer and a bag of potato chips. After all, this is the reason most people ride — to be able to eat all the snacks you want without looking like a blimp.

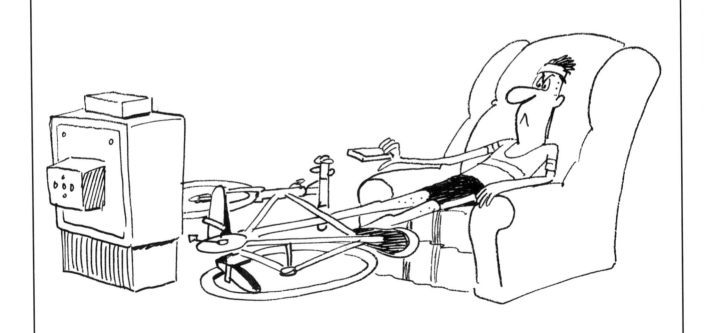

Bike Shoes & Cleats

Bike shoes have these plastic lumps on the bottom that make you walk like a duck when you get off the bike. This is to make you feel like a fool (along with the tight bike pants) when going into a fast food place.

"'Bout 8 Miles."

"Gregg has become so ecologically aware.
He rides his bike everywhere."

"This carbon fiber baby weighs under 19 lbs."

Why Bike Clothes Are So Tight

The manufacturers claim that bike clothes are tight to provide an aerodynamic advantage. Hogwash. The real reason for the tight pants is to show a positive outline of your sex organs. This enables the cyclist to prove these parts are still in approximate working order after all those hours scrunched up on a hard narrow bike seat.

"We just ride to relax."

"I thought yeast infections came from peeing in the woods."

Problems with early Mountain Bikes

Why Bike Pants Are Black

Bike pants are usually black so you can wipe greasy hands on them, without it showing after putting your chain back on. Anyone wearing another color, especially a man, will be suspect at any bike shop, if you get my drift.

"This hill is a bitch."

"These Backroad tours really support their riders."

Things That Go Thunk, Thunk, Thunk

Why is there always something going thunk, thunk, thunk on my bike, a reader writes. While a bike is a simple device, it is also a very dirty and greasy one. No one wants to fix it 'cause your hands get so dirty and then you'll never get a date Saturday night! It's simply easier to put up with the thunking noise.

"I heard it, too."

"Well if it makes you numb, why do you
have to ride so much?"

"Meatloaf again for dinner, pass it on."

"These pit stops don't do Gino's time
one bit of good."

Bike Seats

Why are bike seats uncomfortable? This is a matter of efficiency.
While the country that invented the Lazy Boy recliner surely
could come up with a more comfortable bike seat, your pedaling
efficiency would suffer. You see, you want all the up and down
motion of your feet to go directly to the pedals, not to
compressing the foam rubber under your tush.

Bike Seats

Some racers actually have their seats surgically attached to their ass bone. I'm not making this up. While this makes it much harder to travel by car or plane, they do win bike races.

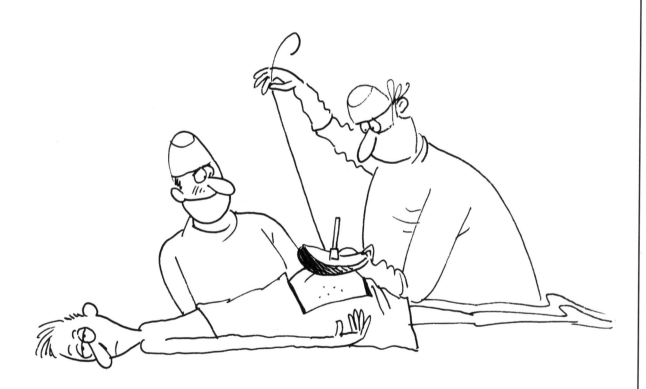

"Mario's eating garlic again."

"Oh my, you should have seen the big one
that just got away."

Why People Buy Mountain Bikes

It's a fact. Most mountain bikes never see a mountain, much less an off road scene. People buy these bikes so they can sit upright and be comfortable and see something rather than be bent over and able to view only their front tire and three inches of road. More chiropractors have been put out of business by mountain bikes than by any other reason.

"I think it's time to go back."

"So I figured, who wants to wear a helmet
in this hot weather."

These other books are available at many fine stores.

#2350 Sailing. Using the head at night • Sex & Sailing • Monsters in the Ice Chest • How to look nautical in bars and much more nautical nonsense.

#2351 Computers. Where computers really are made • How to understand computer manuals without reading them • Sell your old $2,000,000 computer for $60 • Why computers are always lonely and much more solid state computer humor.

#2352 Cats. Living with cat hair • The advantages of kitty litter • Cats that fart • How to tell if you've got a fat cat.

#2353 Tennis. Where do lost balls go? • Winning the psychological game • Catching your breath • Perfecting wood shots.

#2354 Bowling. A book of bowling cartoons that covers: Score sheet cheaters • Boozers • Women who show off • Facing your team after a bad box and much more.

#2355 Parenting. Understanding the Tooth Fairy • 1000 ways to toilet train • Informers and tattle tales • Differences between little girls and little boys • And enough other information and laughs to make every parent wet their beds.

#2356 Fitness. T-shirts that will stop them from laughing at you • Earn big money with muscles • Sex and Fitness • Lose weight with laughter from this book.

#2357 Golf. Playing the psychological game • Going to the toilet in the rough • How to tell a real golfer • Some of the best golf cartoons ever printed.

#2358 Fishing. Handling 9" mosquitoes • Raising worms in your microwave oven • Neighborhood targets for fly casting practice • How to get on a first name basis with the Coast Guard plus even more.

#2359 Bathrooms. Why people love their bathroom • Great games to help pass the time on toilets • A frank discussion of bathroom odors • Plus lots of other stuff everyone out of diapers should know.

#2360 Biking. Why the wind is always against you • Why bike clothes are so tight • And lots of other stuff about what goes thunk, thunk, thunk when you pedal.

#2361 Running. How to "go" in the woods • Why running shoes cost more than sneakers • Keeping your lungs from bursting by letting the other guy talk.

Ivory Tower Publishing Co., Inc.   125 Walnut St., PO Box 9132, Watertown, MA 02272-9132
Telephone #: (617) 923-1111   Fax #: (617) 923-8839